BRITAIN'S HERITAGE

Traction Engines

Anthony Coulls

AMBERLEY

Acknowledgements

Photographs are by the author and Peter Coulls, archive images are from the collections of the author and Hedd Jones; the cutaway diagram of *Oliver* is reproduced by kind permission of the Wheeler family and the cover photograph of a 1925 Burrell Special Scenic Showman's Engine is by Nick Wright. Thanks to Peter Coulls and Hedd Jones for proof-reading the text. This book is dedicated to Dad, Trevor Daw, John Plaister, Dick Blenkinsop, Jack Marshall, Arthur and Hylbert Smith and their ilk – who introduced me to the world of road steam – and to my daughters, Isobel and Charlotte, who show every sign on taking that interest into the next generation.

First published 2017

Amberley Publishing
The Hill, Stroud
Gloucestershire, GL5 4EP

www.amberley-books.com

Copyright © Anthony Coulls, 2017

The right of Anthony Coulls to be identified as the Author of this work has been asserted in accordance with the Copyrights, Designs and Patents Act 1988.

ISBN 978 1 4456 6886 4 (paperback)
ISBN 978 1 4456 6887 1 (ebook)

British Library Cataloguing in Publication Data.
A catalogue record for this book is available from the British Library.

Printed in the UK.

Contents

1
Introduction

What is a traction engine? It's a valid enough question. In the 1960s, there was a fair chance that someone might know what one was. In the twenty-first century, it's possible that a member of the public seeing a traction engine might refer to it as a 'train' – after all, it has smoke coming out of a chimney and makes a similar noise to a railway engine – but it's not a railway engine at all; it's a steam engine that runs on the road and needs no rails. So what is it? What does it do? Why is it called a traction engine? The answer to the last question is fairly simple and the first two questions are what this book is about.

Traction engine comes from the Latin *tractus*, meaning drawn, and the first purpose of such machines was to draw a load behind them. Sometimes they are referred to as road locomotives to distinguish them from railway locomotives – but then also a road locomotive became a development of the simple traction engine too, as we shall see.

Thousands of traction engines were made, along with their derivatives, and found use all over the world; from the prairies of the United States of America to the Siberian steppes. Our concern in this book is the English traction engine, its development, and uses. There's

Oldberrow Rectory – how it all began for me. The author's personal interest is summed up in this photo of Oldberrow Rectory in Warwickshire. The two engines are a Ransomes general purpose engine, *The Countryman*, and Burrell showman's engine *Nero*, owned by Jack Marshall and Arthur and Hylbert Smith respectively, and both engines and men were greatly influential in encouraging my interest in traction engines as a small boy in the 1970s.

Above: What a traction engine should look like. The late John Plaister's Marshall engine at his wake in Swindon in May 2015. John rescued it from scrap in the 1950s and ran it until his death. It is now owned and shown by Carl Brown.

Below: An engine out of time. Alex and Rosy Hayward's Marshall dates from 1893, but the design goes back twenty years before that. Its short wheelbase makes it very manoeuvrable in farmyards. It's currently on loan to the author and family and is seen in West Durham in October 2016.

also a look at the people who used them, where they were made, and the phenomenon of keeping a traction engine for fun. Steam is now a big player in the leisure market and over 3,000 traction engines, steam rollers and such are held by enthusiasts and museums for posterity. Each weekend during the summer hundreds of workable engines are shown at gatherings – or 'rallies' – across the country and this book seeks to explain a bit more about those engines, both large and small, that can be seen on rally fields and, occasionally, on the road amongst modern traffic.

Why steam and how does it work?

Steam power has been around since classical times, with Hero's *Aleopile* from the first century being a form of steam turbine; albeit as an elaborate toy. So what is steam? It's not the white stuff that comes out of your kettle – that's condensed steam, which is visible. Steam is the gas that is heated boiled water – an invisible vapour that, when restricted and held in a vessel, holds energy that can be harnessed for the generation of mechanical power. At 100 degrees centigrade water boils and gives off the vapour; as temperature rises, the boiling is more rapid and in a closed vessel steam pressure builds. It was this steam pressure that gave rise to the first engines – although the steam pumps of Thomas Savery and Thomas Newcomen utilised the pressure of the atmosphere and a vacuum to drive their machines.

Steam was used to fill a space, or cylinder, and then it was condensed using a jet of cold water, creating a vacuum, and atmospheric pressure drove the piston of the engine down. The piston in Newcomen's engine was connected to a wooden rocking beam, which was then attached to a pump rod actuating the pump itself in a mine situation. The first successful application of this was in Dudley in 1712; Savery's 'Engine to Raise Water by Fire' was from 1698, but used no moving parts. However, the seeds of steam power in the developed world were beginning; coal was cheap, labour was cheap, and the scene was set.

James Watt took on the Newcomen engine, making it more efficient, using the steam on both sides of the piston, and noting that the latent energy in steam had potential as it continued to expand once released into the steam engine cylinder. Once Watt had patented his improvements, the engine could truly be said to be a steam engine and many others tried copying or enhancing the idea and looking into other things that a steam engine might do. Water-pumping engines could also be furnace-blowing engines, but the concept of driving machinery appealed – especially as industrial development took hold and factory owners sought to move away from the unpredictability of water power. Therefore, as the eighteenth century moved on, the thought of turning the engine's up and down – or reciprocating –

Did you know?

In 1769, a French engineer called Nicolas Cugnot created his '*Fardier*'. This was a road carriage fitted with a steam engine and boiler at the front end, intended for use by the French Army. Although heavy and cumbersome to operate, it did actually run and is the first successful steam road vehicle – the present tense is used, for you can still see the '*Fardier*' at the *Musée des Arts et Métiers* in Paris.

Although the Murdoch Flyer was a model, a working full-size version was on display at Market Way, Redruth, in 2012 and now resides at the Moseley Toy and Train Museum in Redruth.

movement into rotary motion gained ground and, in 1780, James Pickard added a crank to a Newcomen engine. Before long, engines were built all over the country for mines, mills and furnaces, and the thought of making them move took off. Beam engines were large, cumbersome things, working on low steam pressure. The pressure was so low that in operating instructions of the time, it was said that if the boiler sprang a leak, it could be plugged with a piece of turf! To make a movable engine, the power unit needed to be light but powerful – enter the concept of high pressure, or strong, steam.

In the United Kingdom, an apprentice of James Watt, William Murdoch, began experimenting with higher pressure steam and applying it to a steam carriage, making a successful model in 1784 and patenting it. His first model can be seen in ThinkTank in Birmingham. Murdoch was dissuaded from developing his steam carriage further by James Watt and his business partner, Matthew Boulton, having allegedly frightened the vicar of Redruth with it one dark night. The vicar thought that this thing coming towards him hissing and spitting flame was the Devil come to claim him, so popular legend has it!

Matters rested until the arrival of a Cornishman, Richard Trevithick, in 1801. Trevithick harnessed high pressure steam to make an effective but compact power unit applicable to many purposes – both stationary and moving – and created his 'Puffing Devil'. The machine was so named because the exhaust steam blast up the chimney made a puffing sound. It was mounted on three wheels and needed a team to steer it steadily at the front because of the weight on it, but it worked. One could even claim it was the first powered device to hold a land speed record. Yet the success was short lived – Trevithick and his friends retired to a pub to celebrate their device with a goose dinner but forgot the engine, which ran out of water and exploded! However, the concept of a travelling steam road vehicle had been proven, and a number of passenger carrying road carriages followed, built by Trevithick and a number of other pioneers such as Goldsworthy Gurney. An engine from Gurney's Steam Drag survives and can be seen in Glasgow's Riverside Museum as part of a display, which shows what the larger vehicle would have looked like.

The holder of the land speed record in 1801! This working replica of Trevithick's *Puffing Devil* was built in Cornwall and was seen at the 2008 Trevithick Day in Camborne – an annual event to commemorate the engineer.

English roads still weren't of the best quality, so whilst steam power took off on the railways as the nineteenth century progressed, steam on the road and on the farm was a decade or so behind the iron way. George Stephenson had considered road-going locomotives, but given the power of locomotives at the time and their inability to climb hills, it went no further. Yet, with coal and labour being plentiful and low in cost, steam was never far off the agenda and much satire was made in publications and cartoons of a steam-powered future for the United Kingdom.

2

Origins of the Traction Engine

Trevithick-type engines were the first ones to find use in farm applications, being relatively small but high powered. They were stationary engines though, built into buildings with brick mountings and unable to be easily moved; such as at Erdding, the National Trust property near Wrexham. It wasn't long before the high cost of a steam engine resulted in static engines being supplemented by engines mounted on wheels – portable engines – being developed. These could be moved around from workplace to workplace by horses. A flywheel as part of the engine was used to drive whatever machinery the engine needed to – whether fixed into a building or similarly mobile. It was from one of these that the traction engine was developed; as Thomas Aveling noted, it was a shame to see a steam engine drawn by a team of six horses. However, steam had been tried on a mobile form through the Farmer's Engine, though this had much in common with the railway locomotives of the period, including having its working parts such as the cylinders and connecting rods below the boiler and thus being susceptible to damage from the road or field surface.

Thomas Aveling took a Clayton & Shuttleworth portable engine in 1859 and made it self-moving with a chain drive to the wheels. A horse in shafts still provided the steering at the front, but it wasn't long before mechanical means with either a ship's wheel or tiller were tried. Developments and alterations came thick and fast, with gear drive and worm and gear steering being two major steps forward. The classic shape of the traction engine began to emerge by the late 1860s and, as the nineteenth century progressed, this was refined by designers such as the renowned William Fletcher,

Portable engines were the progenitor of the traction engine as we know it. A self-moving portable was one step away from the complete package. This Marshall portable is owned by the Kearton family and was seen at the Carlisle rally in May 2011.

Early engines drove their wheels by means of a chain before the gear train was developed. No complete engine survives, but these Aveling chain engine remains were exhumed from a Staffordshire coal mine and were displayed at Beamish Museum in September 2010.

In the early years of steam development, all manner of interesting and unconventional machines were built. Records in journals are sometimes all that remains, but can lead on to models being built. This is an 1862 Gillets & Allatt traction engine made by Cherry Hill in recent times and now on display at the Institute of Mechanical Engineers.

who worked for Marshall's of Gainsborough, Davey Paxman of Colchester, and Clayton & Shuttleworth of Lincoln, taking his ideas from place to place. In addition, Fletcher spent time as Works Manager at Burrells of Thetford and was Chief Draughtsman at Wallis & Steevens of Basingstoke, and so was well-placed to write on the subject. He published two texts that are still very readable in 2017 – *Steam on Common Roads* and *English and American Steam Carriages and Traction Engines*; both easily available at affordable prices in the 1970s reprint forms that took place.

What Does a Typical Traction Engine Consist Of?

Boiler – horizontal, multi-tubular 'locomotive' type, with firebox at one end, a barrel with internal fire-tubes passing through a water space in the barrel, and then a smokebox and chimney at the other end. For most traction engines, the boiler doubles up as the main structural member of the vehicle – there is no chassis as such. The firebox sides extend upwards to carry the crankshaft in engines built after the 1870s and are known as hornplates.

Cylinder – or cylinders – the first engines were simple, single cylinder machines, but twin cylinders gave double the power and easier starting and smoother motion. Then, with an eye on efficiency, various compounding systems were developed, where the exhaust steam from one high pressure cylinder got used in a second, larger low-pressure cylinder to maximise the use of the energy in the steam. A piston in the cylinder was driven backwards and forwards with the in and out governed by a valve. Depending on the shape of the valve, they were either slide or piston valves – titles which can be heard today when describing traction engines. It was here that the power rating of an engine was described in nominal horsepower – most traction engines being five, six, seven or eight nominal horsepower, based on the diameter of the cylinder, pressure, and length of piston stroke. The actual horsepower is more like eight to ten times the nominal figure.

The classic shape of a traction engine began to emerge in the 1870s, and Barry Woods' massive Aveling typifies that. It attended the Masham Rally in July 2015.

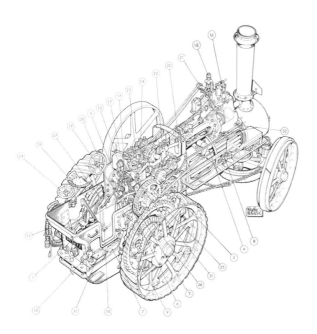

A cutaway diagram of Ruston & Hornsby traction engine *Oliver*, drawn by the late Geoff Wheeler.

Motion – the arrangement of piston rod, connecting rod and crankshaft, plus the associated eccentrics, rods, straps and links that control the working of the slide or piston valve. These are usually also adjustable so that the engine can be reversed or 'notched up', which makes more use of the expansive power of steam and makes the engine more efficient.

Gears and shafts – this is the drive train from crankshaft to driving axle. Most traction engines have two sliding gears on the crankshaft that can be engaged by sliding them in and out of mesh with the crankshaft. These give two speeds of travel. The motion, flywheel, and actual engine itself can be disengaged from either gear so that the flywheel can be used to drive machinery or equipment with the traction engine in use as a static power source. In static form, most engines also had a centrifugal governor that allowed the engine to run at a constant speed despite fluctuations in the need for power; when sawing, for example. Road locomotives and tractors also had springing set up in the drive train to give a better ride and less shock from the road through the engine itself. Drive from the back axle to the wheels was achieved by two removable driving pins and a driving plate, which locked one to the other. Many engines had a winch drum and cable fastened to the back axle – removal of the driving pins allowed the back axle to rotate independently from the wheels and, thus, the winch could be operated; a very useful tool indeed for the ever-versatile traction engine!

Wheels – most engines had four; two small at the front and two large driven wheels at the back. There were variations on the theme, some engines being four-wheel drive experiments in the late nineteenth century and then other differences such as wide Fenland wheels for engines in the softer country. Steel or iron wheels had cross members diagonally bolted or riveted on – called strakes – to give grip and traction, with bolt-on spuds or cleats to give extra traction in muddy or icy conditions.

Steering – the earliest engines were steered by horses in shafts and then tillers or ships'-type steering wheels mounted at the front of the engine, away from the driver, so communication was difficult between himself and the steersman. In the 1860s the steersman joined the driver on the footplate, with steering via gears and chains to the

A convertible engine could be both a roller and a general purpose engine and be changed between versions. Here's a McLaren of Leeds convertible, showing the flange at the front end to which the roller parts could be bolted, seen at a Tyseley Steam Centre open day in 1969. This engine had not long been imported from Ireland by the Revd Fred Coley of Webheath, Redditch, Worcestershire.

front axle. A variation of this was the early Fowler ploughing engines with what became known as 'tank' steering and, due to the heavy steering, low gearing was necessary and the arrangement required the steersman to turn the wheel to the left when he wanted to go right and vice versa!

Water and coal tender – a riveted box on the back of the engine where the driver stood to access the controls, with coal in a bunker behind and water in the tank beneath. Some road engines and tractors had an auxiliary water tank under the boiler, known as a belly tank.

Controls – the basics were forward/reverse lever and regulator to control steam (also speed). Additionally there were devices to put water into the boiler, an injector, and a pump. To measure steam and water levels, other gauges were also fitted. Some engines had brakes, but not all! The brake acted on either the back axle or flywheel and was aimed to slow the engine but not necessarily stop it; the actual act of stopping was usually achieved by pulling the reversing lever back towards its mid point – the equivalent of neutral on a car. The same action could be used for slowing the engine on a hill. Drain cocks were also fitted to allow condensation to be cleared from the cylinder(s) at the start of the day or after a prolonged period of standing, for water cannot be compressed, and any trapped water in the cylinder with the engine in motion could cause serious damage.

Very few engines were fitted with whistles in their working lives as the law of the time precluded it; audible warnings to other road users were given with bells or gongs instead, especially on the small, faster steam tractors. To avoid scaring horses, many road-going engines also had side sheets or motion covers to hide the various rods from sight. Thus, the only sign an engine was in motion was the turning flywheel, but, again on road engines and tractors, the flywheel was either plated or solid to ensure that the flashing of spokes was not seen by anything that may have taken fright at seeing them.

Many agricultural engines had water lifters – a device allowing them to suck water up a hose from a stream, pond or trough, using steam pressure to create the vacuum effect. Whilst effective, one had to beware of the quality of the water or the legality of taking it. Extracting water from a horse drinking trough wasn't really on. Brackish water could lead to steaming difficulties or boiler problems. As a result, a lot of road-going steam engines carried a plate on the footplate saying to wash the boiler out every 100 hours or fourteen working days – this kept the boiler plates clean and lessened damage through silt and scale build-up.

Canopy/awning – engines were often fitted with roofs; these could cover half of the engine, three quarters of it, or run the whole length – from tender to front of the chimney. Some were works-fitted, others made locally by joiners or the engine's operator. All these different details could change the look of an engine significantly, and in some cases allowed the knowledgeable viewer to tell either the make of the engine or who it belonged to – a real skill indeed!

Variations on a theme formed the different types of traction engine that feature in this book; the ploughing engine, steam tractor, road locomotive, and showman's engine. Steam rollers and steam wagons and lorries also have their origin in the same basic layout, but are beyond the scope of our coverage in this book.

Size and weight varied as well. Small steam tractors were made down to three tons to get round punitive legislation on what the law called 'locomotives and heavy motor cars', and some ploughing engines weighed in at over twenty tons. The vast majority of traction engines were in the rough area of eight to twelve tons in general, with steam tractors settling at five tons or so. The smallest tractor could easily be driven by one person and would fit in a modern domestic garage; the big ploughing engines or road locomotives would tower above such a machine and require a purpose built shed to be kept in. In general, the layout remained the same, apart from some of the later attempts at steam tractors to be serious competition to the internal combustion opposition.

One of the oldest McLaren traction engines in existence lives in Ireland. Works number 60, now named *Seana Mac*, came over to the 2010 Great Dorset Steam Fair, which had a McLaren theme.

3
Steam on the Land

Threshing, Sawing, Baling, Ploughing, Dredging and Cultivating

During the late eighteenth and early nineteenth centuries, steam engine technology diffused through the mining and manufacturing centres of industrialising Britain. Only later, from the 1840s, did farm workers and country people become familiar with steam-powered devices. Traction engines were particularly important, for they could pull specialised machinery or heavy loads between farms. Once there, they acted as stationary local power sources, driving devices such as threshing machines with a belt from the flywheel. These engines were the self-moving descendants of earlier 'portable' steam engines, which were drawn to the working site by horses on their own (un-driven) wheels as noted earlier. But once the steam engine could move itself, it acquired new potential. Traction engines could deploy their enormous power to haul out tree stumps, create land drains, and many other tasks. Specialised variants – ploughing engines – worked in pairs equipped with cable drums that drew a plough back and forth between them.

The traction engine – fitted with a governor device to ensure constant speed and power – was incredibly versatile. It could drive the threshing machine and also a baler for the straw, which was the by-product of the threshing. It could drive large rack saw benches to convert

A late threshing scene, but one typical of an activity that could be seen for well over a century across the country. A Burrell general purpose engine provides the power and the picture can only be dated as there is a petrol tractor to the edge of the image.

A versatile Tasker steam tractor – which is convertible between steam tractor and roller – engaged in stone crushing at the Strawberries & Steam event, Lotmead, in June 2013; sadly an event that no longer happens.

Steam sawing at Lotmead, June 2013 – almost an industrial scale process on occasion with a Ransomes portable engine providing the power.

round timber into usable planks and small saw benches to cut logs for firewood. Away from the farm, the engine could run a stone crusher and then haul the crushed stone to where it was required. Traction engines were generally slow on the road, which is where the development of the road locomotive came in for haulage, but the traction engine never fully lost the purpose of drawing a load – whether it was tree trunks or a trailer of beets.

What we call a traction engine today was marketed as a 'general purpose engine'; typically suitable for the farmer or large estate, it also became popular with agricultural contractors who pulled a threshing outfit from farm to farm. A threshing outfit consisted of the engine, the threshing machine, a straw elevator, and sometimes a chaff cutter. It travelled with its team during the autumn, winter and spring months, the team consisting of a driver and a man to feed the threshing machine, supplemented by farm hands. It was the responsibility

This late build (1932) Ransomes, Sims & Jefferies Ltd agricultural engine is displayed at Market Bosworth steam engine rally in 1969, when owned by John Vernon of Newbold Vernon, Leicestershire. It was the last compound engine built by Ransomes and was attached to a threshing drum from the same manufacturer.

of the farmer to provide coal, water, and unskilled labour to assist with the operation. The summer months tended to be when such gear found use in sawing and haulage, and thus the tackle was never idle.

Steam ploughing was initially a failure – early agricultural engines were too heavy to draw a plough directly, and this is where the history books' claim that steam played no real part in agriculture begins. However, the 1850s and 1860s was a great period of innovation and experimentation; if you can't take the steam engine across the land, why not use its ability to drive a winch to then pull a plough or cultivating implement over the area? Some complex systems of pulleys, anchors, rope and a plough were established to a degree of success. In 1861, a Wiltshire Quaker called John Fowler devised a two-engine system, which was faster and more effective, using two traction engines with a rope drum underneath each one to pull a plough across a field between them using a wire rope. The ploughs could give up to five or seven furrows at a time. At the end of each crossing of the field, the engines would advance another plough length. This is where the steam ploughing set came into its own, ploughing much larger areas much faster than any other form of technology at the time. Being a massive investment, ploughing engines tended, like threshing sets, to be owned by contractors or farmers with very large acreage. The two-engine system went global though, across Europe and even into Africa and Australia. The system could be applied to other earth-moving equipment too, including cultivators and mole drainers, where the power of the engines could deal with difficult ground that horses could not cope with.

At the September 2016 50th Anniversary working for the Steam Plough Club at York, Richard Vernon showed his rebuilt Howard roundabout ploughing system. Whilst the engine is original, the rest of the gear – windlass, plough and self moving anchors – are recreations copied from originals in Australia and from pictures.

A model of an early Fowler twin-engine ploughing system used to be displayed in the former Agriculture Gallery at the Science Museum in London.

A typical 1870s Fowler single ploughing engine was on display at the 2011 Shrewsbury Steam Rally at Onslow Park. It has been rebuilt by a later owner, and displays what is known as an Allen pattern chimney compared to the plain stovepipe it would have been built with.

The classic twentieth-century Fowler compound ploughing engine looks like this, and hundreds were made for home use and abroad. A good number have survived into preservation and are demonstrated each year. This one was at the 50th Anniversary celebrations for the Steam Plough Club in 2016.

A further use of the ploughing engine was in the dredging of lakes and estuaries – another job for the contractor, and a hard filthy job; pulling a scoop of silt from the water course to land for emptying. The major Midlands contractor Bomford & Evershed used their ploughing engines for cultivation, dredging, and drainage works across the Midlands and further afield. They did major earthworks around a river estuary at Tywyn in Mid-Wales, which must have been a sight to see. During the Second World War, a handful of steam ploughing engines in

Did you know?

In the Second World War, two Fowler ploughing engines were adapted to play a part in the 'Pipe Line under the Ocean' (PLUTO) project to run oil pipelines across the English Channel to assist with the Normandy landings in Northern France. The engines were used to pull the pipelines ashore in France with their slow and steady power, but high torque.

Yorkshire found a further, diverse use as emergency winders at coal mines in case the main shaft winding engines were incapacitated by enemy action.

The end of steam began with the rise of internal combustion after the First World War, extra mechanisation in the form of light cheap tractors, and the development of the combine harvester, which was, in essence, a self-propelled threshing machine. Such equipment did not require large gangs to look after it or long hours to get it ready. The petrol tractor was faster and less labour and cost-heavy as a pair of ploughing engines, and steam power lost out to the power of pounds, shillings, and pence. It could plough directly with a plough behind it across the land, and use a power take off or driving pulley to run a threshing machine, saw bench or baler, and be turned off instantly at the end of the day. Whilst there were attempts to make successful steam tractors that could challenge the petrol machines – and some of these were very worthwhile – it was too little too late and few were made or sold.

Steam threshing or ploughing tackle dispersal sales in the 1930s usually ended in the machinery going for scrap, however well-maintained, and the wholesale scrap drive of the Second World War saw engines change hands for destruction at £25! Hundreds of engines ended their days as stationary steam boilers, either used at nurseries for sterilising soil or in farms for boiling down pig swill – tasks that saw a number of engines cling to life long enough to be saved by enthusiasts.

As the competition for steam from the petrol tractor grew, some engine builders looked for alternatives to move away from the costly twin-engine ploughing system. Fodens of Sandbach created the Agritractor to try direct ploughing with. Lightweight and with an enclosed engine, it was effective, but too late to stem the flow of the internal combustion engine. September 2016 saw the sole survivor in the UK engaged once again in direct ploughing at York.

A Fowler ploughing engine with side drum for dredging made an unusual sight at Rempstone in September 2006 for the Steam Plough Club's 40th anniversary 'Great Challenge'.

Steam is today widely seen as outmoded, and it is true that the technical development of the steam engine in agriculture really ended around the First World War. Despite this, it died a lingering death commercially from the 1920s; declining rapidly throughout the 1930s and 1940s, and dying out finally in the 1950s to early 1960s. Odd users still remained – the farmer using his ploughing tackle once a year or using his engine and drum to thresh in the autumn – but as a major source of power, steam was finished before the Second World War. Despite this, the last pair of working ploughing engines used for dredging only entered preservation in the early years of the twenty-first century. For the person used to seeing shiny, glossy engines on rally fields, to see this pair at work on an estate with filthy brass and chained to large trees as anchors was to see steam in the raw – a rare link with bygone times as the crews lived in living vans near to the job and worked in hard conditions, having to maintain the engines on the job. I saw them on an estate near Ludlow in the mid-1990s and it was a privilege to see something that was just clinging to survival, but would have been commonplace sixty years earlier. We are nostalgic and sentimental about engines now, but so often forget that they were pieces of machinery to serve a purpose; tools to do a job.

4
Steam on the Common Road and in Industry

Haulage by Road Locomotives and Steam Tractors, Long and Short Distance

After the agricultural engine proved its worth, engine builders began developing steam-powered road locomotives to take advantage of the power of steam to go further and faster than the normal traction engine, and with greater economy too. Although of various sizes, they shared a high level of specification, including three gears (as opposed to the one or two gears of agricultural engines), fully sprung axles, and extra water tanks – known as 'belly tanks' – mounted under the boiler barrel.

These developments increased the speed of the engines from the usual seven to eight miles per hour to between ten and fifteen miles per hour. They also increased the range in terms of needing water, which increased from ten to fifteen miles to twenty-five to thirty miles. Road locomotives followed a twin cylinder layout known as a double crank compound. High-pressure steam was fed into a small cylinder and then exhausted into a second, larger cylinder to create more efficient use of steam, and to make use of the latent energy that remained and usually got wasted up the chimney in the form of an engine's

The equivalent of a heavy goods vehicle special load today, Pickfords' road steam ensemble is on the move on an unknown date transporting a massive casting – quite some undertaking in the late 1930s.

chuff! The road locomotive could be used on its own or in harness with other engines to move large loads of all kinds; railway locomotives, blocks of stone, ship propellers, even the Great Peter bell were moved by steam. Engines could be owned by a single contractor or a company with a fleet, and names such as Norman E. Box and Road Engines & Kerr or Coulsons became well-known for their work transporting boilers, transformers, and other large pieces of equipment – often over long and hard journeys. Box's engines finished their lives with Pickfords, but the great days of steam haulage were over by the Second World War – much as large internal combustion tractors came upon the scene and required fewer men to operate them. Economically, the damage was done by the 1933 Salter Report and its subsequent partial implementation in the 1934 Road Traffic Act and the 1935 Budget. Road transport was made to pay its way, taxed on the notional damage done to the road. Steam engines with high unladen weight therefore were essentially taxed-off the road for haulage.

Oddities in the road locomotive world were the Thomson road steamers, created by Robert William Thomson in Scotland. These were fitted with rubber tyres and a vertical boiler and tested extensively in the UK. Unorthodox in appearance, they nevertheless performed well and were made under licence in the 1860s and 1870s by Burrells of Thetford, Tennants of Leith, Ransomes, Sims & Head of Ipswich, and Robey of Lincoln. They were exported internationally and made their name in India with Colonel Crompton, the noted engineer whose family firm became the electrical giant Crompton-Parkinson. Whilst the Thomson road steamers faded out after their designer's death in 1871, some remained in use well into the twentieth century; but the adventures of their creator and operators paved the way for widespread use of road locomotives as the years passed.

A versatile Tasker tractor and load demonstrating how its work is very similar to the twenty-first century 'man and van' concept – something that was not lost on the manufacturers, whose image this was. Used to promote sales, the steam tractor was a very versatile machine.

The reality of working steam: Fowler tractor 19890 working for Olive & Partington papermakers in Glossop goods yard sometime before the Second World War – no gloss and shine here!

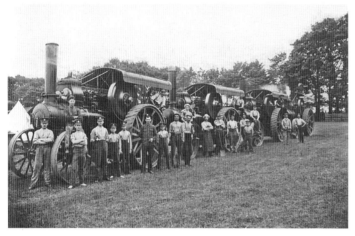

A line-up of Fowler road locomotives with their crews ready for military service. Before tracked tanks and light petrol lorries, they were the only means of transporting heavy materials on the field of conflict.

Steam haulage found many uses and after a long life in Africa, a Boer War veteran Fowler B5 road locomotive is now a prized showpiece in Northumberland and was shown at Beamish Museum in April 2016.

Road locomotives gained smaller cousins after the 1903 Motor Car Act. The Act allowed the manufacture of steam engines – called steam tractors – up to a five-ton limit. They were really small road locomotives and used for the same purpose (but were lighter and faster), with belly tanks, side plates to the motion, and disc fly wheels to avoid frightening the horses. This opened up the possibility of light and fast haulage across the country – a steam tractor and trailer or van became the equivalent of a Transit van for many. Attempts were made with degrees of success to use steam tractors on direct ploughing as well, but it was their haulage capability and speed on the road for which the steam tractor found favour. Both road locomotives and steam tractors were used extensively by the military, initially in the Boer War, but also in the First World War.

Did you know?

A celebrity steam tractor is the 3-ton *Horse's Friend*, bought by two ladies who lived at Crystal Palace to pull loads up the hill outside their home and relieve the horses that pulled such loads. It is said that some horses grew used to the sight of the engine, which would take their carts and thus they would stop until the engine came to take their load to the top of the hill. Ownership of the engine passed to the Royal Society for the Prevention of Cruelty to Animals, and now in preservation, the engine still bears the initials RSPCA on the show fields it attends.

The famous 3-ton Taskers tractor of 1903 known as *The Horses Friend* is seen on 24 August 2014 in Onslow Park outside Shrewsbury, at a long established rally organised by County of Salop Steam Engine Society.

The adaptability of the steam engine is seen in F. H. Rogers of Basingstoke's Fowler K7 ploughing engine. It has been fitted with a crane jib to the tender to allow it to undertake lifting as well as winching.

Heavy haulage in the North East – the Fowler road locomotive *Providence* shows how it was done, only this picture was taken in 2016 at Beamish Museum.

A number of manufacturers built tractors that could be converted to rollers and back again. This 5-ton Marshall tractor *Mascot* at Blythe Bridge in September 2013 is one of them. It also worked at one time for a showman, but no twisted brass or dynamo for this piece of equipment.

The steam tractor was the equivalent of a Transit van or dumper truck, and could prove useful in a number of applications – here's a Fowler tractor with a pantechnicon in removal van mode.

'My glory is in hauling and lighting the fair' – so runs the wording on the side boards of the canopy of a Garrett steam tractor now preserved in the Netherlands. And so it was. The traction engine could be a mundane piece of haulage equipment, but it found favour with showmen around the country in the form of the steam tractor and road locomotive. The versatility of engines showed again as, once the load – usually fairground rides in dismantled form in packing trucks, or circus trailers and living vans – had been set up, the engine was set to a secondary use. With the showman's engine or tractor, this was usually in the form of providing electricity for the fair – either for lighting the attractions or rides from a steam tractor, or generating electricity to drive the rides themselves from a dynamo at the front of a road locomotive. As rides developed, got bigger and more complex, the need for extra power resulted in the Special Scenic engine being developed. This was a speciality of Burrells, who built a number of engines with what was called an exciter dynamo mounted behind the engine chimney to enhance the electric field from the original dynamo. Why 'Scenic'? The big rides that needed this extra power were what were called 'Scenic Railways' or switchback rides with powered cars, whereas many earlier rides were mechanically driven from a central engine or a single electric motor. A different variation of the showman's engine was built by Savage of Kings Lynn – makers of fairground rides and engineers – when they created an engine that was also capable of driving the ride, having had the ride built up around it. It also had a small engine fitted to the front end to drive the organ on the ride. A very complex machine, very few were made, though a full size replica is being constructed in Kent by an enthusiast.

The earliest showman's engines were simply road locomotives for haulage, as seen with George Baker's very early Burrell. It was supposedly later converted to a centre engine for Baker and Cain's Gallopers but no photographs can be found to evidence this.

Just at the end of the 1930s, the Burrell Showman's *Gladiator* owned by F. Gray of Pinner was still a common sight on the road pulling a set of gallopers in their packing trucks. The ride centre engine is immediately behind the engine. *Gladiator* found further work on demolition jobs in London in the Second World War.

Foden weren't as prolific as Burrells or Fowlers for showman's engines but made a very creditable engine, as this image from the 1906 catalogue shows.

On a modern-day rally field, you can tell the showman's engines – they are the finely decorated engines, usually painted maroon and yellow with twisted brass supports to the canopy and lit bulbs around the edge. Whilst it is true that many showman operators did indeed make their engines as ornate as possible (and tried to outdo each other!), the large numbers of lamps would not have been commonplace as all the electricity would have been required for the ride or sideshow, and there would only have been a few bulbs above the engine's motion to illuminate it whilst working. Showman's engines worked very hard and long hours, from setting up and knocking down the fair, to travelling antisocial hours to get to the next town for set up. Doing so, they needed large lamps to light the way ahead. As they were basically road locomotives, they had springs, compounding, auxiliary water tanks, and sometimes three speeds to enhance their ability to travel between locations. Contemporary accounts of setting up for St Giles' Fair in Oxford tell of races down Beaumont Street in the desire to gain the best pitch for the large attractions. Some engines were fitted with what were called 'feast cranes' as well to assist in the erecting and dismantling of rides using a jib attached to the rear of the engine and cable from the winch drum. Maintenance was often done on the road, though some larger operators had yards where work was carried out in the closed winter season. The famous showman Pat Collins of Bloxwich latterly had engines maintained by a local foundry and engineering works to ensure his engines were in peak condition.

The Fowler showman's engine *Renown* was one of two built for John Murphy of Newcastle, turned out in blue without ornamentation or brightwork. 'Plain but Powerful' was the motto, and the engine returned to the North East in November 2009 to be paired with the set of gallopers that are based at the Beamish Museum.

Left: Burrell *Wait and See*, Bloxwich, August 2009. Not all showman's engines were maroon – this Burrell *Wait and See* was finished in yellow and white for reasons now lost in time. In preservation, it carries these colours again; not the most practical, but certainly eye-catching, as here at the Pat Collins 150th anniversary event at Bloxwich, August 2009.

Below: *The Leader*, a Foster showman's road locomotive built in 1921, once in the ownership of amusement caterer Pat Collins. It is shown in the yard of Hunt Bros Foundry, Oldbury, during a visit by members of the Road Locomotive Society in May 1987.

Burrells of Thetford turned out *Ex-Mayor* – a double crank compound showman's road locomotive – for G. T. Tuby in 1925. It is shown in blue at the Bedfordshire Steam & Country Fayre, Old Warden Park, September 2011.

Steam on the fair was really a preserve of the 1890s to late 1930s, and most showman's engines were made by Fowler of Leeds and Burrells of Thetford, with Foster of Lincoln making up the rest of the significant numbers and eight other manufacturers building a handful of the 400-plus that were built new. Road locomotives were also converted in their commercial lives, most notably by Charles Openshaw of Reading. Customers had favourites; George Tuby of Doncaster favouring Burrells, all painted in Great Eastern Railway deep blue, which set them apart from other engines on the fairground.

Did you know?

George T. Tuby was a prominent local politician and the names of his engines reflected that career – from '*Councillor*' and '*Alderman*' right through to '*Mayor*' and the slightly sadly named '*Ex-Mayor*'.

Showman's tractors came from Garretts of Leiston, Aveling & Porter, Fowlers, and a handful from other makers. The last new Showman's engine was built in 1934 and by the 1950s very few were left; the last commercially used engines being some of those from the Collins stable in the West Midlands *circa* 1956.

Did you know?

During the Second World War, a number of showman's engines found alternative employment on war work. In bomb-damaged towns and cities, the powerful showman's engine with its winch came into its own on demolition tasks. The wire rope was attached to ruined buildings and the engine used to pull down the remains for clearance of the bomb sites. Hard and dangerous work, but the engines and their crews rose to the challenge.

5
The Engine Builders

Traction engines were made all across the country, though very few were Scots-built and none were made in Wales. There were various reasons as to why an individual user might chose a Foster from Lincoln over a Marshall from Gainsborough. Often cost was a major factor, but so was location and the expense of delivery. Some farmers or contractors stuck with engines or companies out of loyalty, but in the case of a successful design such as the twin-engine ploughing system, whilst other manufacturers tried hard, it was Fowler of Leeds who led the field and made many more than any other builder. Likewise, although not strictly traction engines but in terms of associated equipment, many more Foster or Marshall threshing machines were made than those by any other makers.

Fowlers had a reputation for solidity and good Yorkshire engineering, and Burrells had style and craftsmanship, going back to the days when form and function went together. The design of engines and ease of working had a lot to do with their desirability. An eminent designer of traction engines was William Fletcher, who worked for Marshalls, Clayton &

Paxman's Improved General Purpose Traction Engines.

This illustration shows the Gearing Side of Paxman's Single Cylinder Agricultural Locomotive.

Prices and Particulars on application.

646

Though Davey Paxman didn't make as many traction engines as a number of other makers, their product was simple yet elegant and did the job well, as this trade card shows.

A works photo of a 6 nominal horsepower Garrett shows the detail to which the builders went to turn out engines for their official portrait. Usually the background was painted out of the negative or was a white sheet.

Shuttleworth and Davey Paxman. His engines were reckoned to be good-lookers that could perform too. And whilst looks were not a prime consideration, owners could specify colours, chimney tops and other details – or omit details altogether for cheapness. The author has enjoyed a period looking after an 1893 Marshall that was built for Isaac Ball, a Lancashire contractor; the engine has no handbrake, no springs, no whistle and no fripperies at all – it is a basic machine built to do a job and built down to a price. Another surviving Marshall built around the same time has all the above accoutrements, plus a flywheel brake and other niceties. Current engine crews do enjoy having a go on the old Marshall, but they are always keen to give it back at the end of the day! It gives an interesting insight into the world of working steam, when one would have to deal with this every day, on steep hills and with a load behind the tender.

Engineering in the Provinces – The Rural Steam Manufacturing Business
In the nineteenth century, engineering centres appeared in industrial locations – Sheffield, Birmingham, Manchester, Leeds, and London to name a few. But amongst them were some more unusual places, such as Thetford, Kings Lynn, and Rochester; the city of Lincoln provided a base for four engineering companies. Why were these anomalies there? The answer is

agricultural engineering and in the nineteenth century, this quite often meant steam engines in the form of traction engines.

The producers of the steam engines used mostly in mines and factories were based in the leading urban centres, but most traction engine producers for agricultural use were located in rural centres. Eastern England, with larger, flatter and drier farms, was home to most of the better-known makers. Traction engine manufacture eventually petered out in the 1930s, although some of these firms became the lorry and truck makers of the recent past. In spite of much attention to individual manufacturers from enthusiasts, the way in which expertise in steam engineering and manufacture was developed in these rural centres, and how these rural producers acquired their engineering expertise, has hitherto been unexplored.

A few companies – like John Fowler, in Leeds – were embedded in a rich engineering and manufacturing environment. Most, though, were remote from industrial areas and many – like Burrells of Thetford – were the only (or the main) engineering concern in a small or mid-sized market town. Some – for example, Richard Garrett and Sons in Leiston, Suffolk – were isolated 'engineering islands' buried deep in agricultural country.

Did you know?

The Garrett 'Long Shop' is now a museum, which claims the building as 'one of the earliest purpose-built production lines in existence – made long before Henry Ford had the same idea'.

This image from a Fowler catalogue shows their Hercules tractor, which was developed directly as a response to new legislation from 1920.

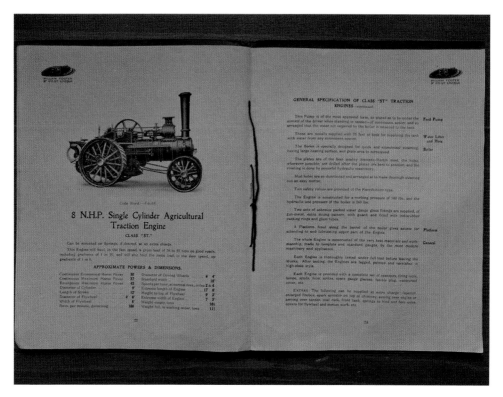

Manufacturers were at pains to point out every advantage of their engines, as this Foster 8 nhp catalogue entry shows.

The products of the provincial firms were beautifully made and were both deployed in Britain and sold around the world, achieving extraordinarily long working lives. They often embodied sophisticated features – for example, compounding of the engine cycle (multiple cylinders working at successively lower pressures to improve efficiency). However, at the time traction engine makers were flourishing, it is generally held that the centres of excellence in stationary steam engine design were the firms in Birmingham, Manchester and (still to a certain extent) London.

So did these country makers rely on peripatetic engineers from these important steam engineering centres to help them develop their engines? It is possible that there was a diffusion of steam engine expertise spreading out through provincial England from the traditional Midlands and Northern locations for steam engine manufacture. The engine man in *Tess of the D'Urbervilles* 'spoke in a strange northern accent', but there is little collated evidence for the origins of agricultural steam engineers. One designer, William Fletcher, did, as we have seen, move between several firms, but better surveys of the career paths of nineteenth-century steam engineers would be immensely useful, as would 'destination surveys' of 'alumni' from firms such as Boulton and Watt – other frontline steam engine makers. This could be a subject for future research.

Did you know?

Fosters of Lincoln, well-known for traction engine and steam tractor manufacture, built the first petrol powered tanks for use in the First World War. After the conflict finished, all new Foster steam engines carried the cast image of a tank on the makers' ring fitted to the smokebox door.

Catalogues and literature are nice collectors' pieces. Here are a couple of Foster catalogues and an advertising brochure for a Midlands boiler repairer.

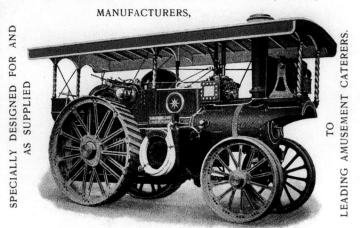

A Burrell trade card appeals directly to the showman and is hand coloured to enhance the attraction.

Of course the diffusion idea may credit far too much to England's well-known Midlands and Northern industrial centres, which had expanded at such an enormous rate from the late eighteenth century. Future research might, perhaps, suggest that such a model undervalues natural human and locally based ingenuity. The long rural tradition of iron working, blacksmithing, and the making of agricultural implements of all kinds could certainly have allowed independent centres of design expertise to arise independently in many separate locations. Local firms could build engines in single figures or handfuls – such as Fysons of Soham – in contrast to the thousands built by Fowlers.

Perhaps the two finest showman's engines ever built were the Fowler *Supreme* and the Burrell *Simplicity* and the works photo of the latter exudes quality. Built for Mrs A. Deakin as Number 4092, it was new in 1930 and almost the last Burrell made – although constructed at Garrett's Leiston works as part of the AGE combine.

6
Working with Steam

What was it like? What did the steam engine mean to people's working lives? Steam threshing contractors and enginemen were itinerant people; the same was true for ploughing gangs, travelling from job to job. This was because steam equipment was inherently expensive and thus for a farmer to invest in buying his own tackle and it spend much of the year idle made no economic sense at all. Thus the steam contractor had a full season of sawing and threshing, or ploughing and cultivation with a bit of dredging thrown in. Some of the larger concerns ran fleets of steam rollers too, to ensure their machinery and men were busy all year – particularly well known was Eddison & De Mattos of Dorchester. To ensure full utilisation of assets, some traction engines were made as convertible machines – so they could change in half a day's work between being a traction engine to a road roller with smooth rolls, but in the end one still had only one engine.

Ploughing gangs could be away for weeks at a time, and thus a living van for the crew became a valued part of the equipment. A ploughing van might have to accommodate six in a degree of comfort. That said, there are stories of some enginemen who were happy to lie in a sheet under a warm engine and go to sleep; needless to say, these did not tend to be

In the years before the First World War, a Fowler single cylinder traction engine arrives at an unknown farm with a threshing machine and portable engine in tow. The driver appears keen for the photographer to be finished whilst farmhands are by the gate waiting to begin setting the machine up.

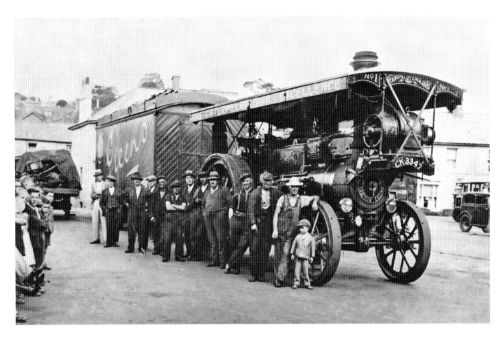

The men of steam are seen with Green's Burrell No. 3089 *His Majesty* just before leaving Newton Abbot fair. The driver and his mate are likely to be the two men in the front of the photo – the rest will be gaff lads and possibly Mr Green himself, standing proud with hands in his pockets by the back wheel.

J. Hickey & Sons were heavy steam haulage contractors based in Richmond, London. One of their engines, *City of London* – a Burrell of 1913 – is seen hauling a large drum for a papermaking company in High Wycombe. The load rating of 30 tons can be seen on the bogie being towed, giving an indication of the weight these engines frequently travelled with across the country.

married men! There was a great spirit of camaraderie amongst ploughing teams – there had to be; from engine men to ploughmen and the cook boy whose job was to keep everyone fed. Ingenuity for the menu was not uncommon and a number of dishes from field finds were usually the thing. The cook boy would gradually work his way up through the team if he was any good and could end up an engine driver after learning the craft for a number of years, and so the cycle continued. A living van was a very unusual addition to a threshing set. Usually the threshing 'round' was local enough to allow the gang to commute by foot or bicycle, with no more than a thirty mile or so radius from home.

Maintenance of the engines varied – from the big contractors such as Allens of Oxford who had well equipped workshops, to the repairs in the field to tired old nineteenth-century engines carried out with wire and a hammer. There is record of complete fireboxes being replaced on occasion by the side of the road and, when one considers that men derived their livelihoods from these engines, it comes as no surprise that they would want their valuable machine back in service as quickly as possible. Axles could break, and another tricky task to undertake was replacing these, as there were no recovery vehicles and the engine owner or driver would be under pressure from the local constabulary to clear the highway. Some drivers were skilled men, trained in the ways of repair and operation and would keep the engines in fine condition throughout the year. It soon became known locally as to who looked after engines and who didn't. Adverts for engine drivers would say 'plug-droppers and bevy 'omey's need not apply'; that is, if you had damaged an engine by dropping the fusible plug or liked a drink, this job was not for you!

Despite the rough men and poor conditions one had to endure, there was pride in the job, and when many engines were pensioned off either in the pre-war period or 1950s, a lot went to the scrap yard for very little money with brass still shining. Often there was a tear in the eye of the contractor who was saying goodbye to a much-loved piece of equipment but, in reality, that was all they were – tools to do a job – and the 1950s had little time for sentimentality in the brave new world of the mechanised farm.

Threshing – or thrashing – was an annual event, looked forward to by many, and a spectacle. The number of photographs of village life where the threshing machine and gang takes

The working day started for many in the yard; some engines were out in the open, others had a shed such as this one in Hampshire seen in October 2009 – though it could easily pass for a century earlier.

Anne Neal's Burrell showman's engine *Victoria* No. 1999 has come to grief at Nuneaton's Easter Fair and work to extract it from its predicament appears to have started.

centre stage gives the evidence to this. It was hard physical work, dusty, and dirty. An extra excitement was often a concentration of rats at the end of the stook as they were driven down to the base of the stook. Trousers were tied at the bottom of the leg to stop the rats going up men's legs, and a graphic and lively description of threshing day is covered in Thomas Hardy's *Tess of the d'Urbervilles*. Even today, there were some people around who remember the last of the commercial steam threshing sets in parts of rural Sussex arriving around noon to set up for two weeks' work threshing six large stooks. This was in the late 1950s and early 1960s – just as steam threshing at rallies and heritage venues began to take off. The author's father and friends set to threshing an eighteen-month-old harvest of winter wheat for 'fun' in Warwickshire in February 1969. Dad reckoned he had never worked so hard or ached so much in his life, but all the gang learned a lot about the working day of a threshing team. Threshing in the twenty-first century is very much done for demonstration at rallies – nowhere more so than the Great Dorset Steam Fair – but a handful of farmers still thresh by steam in the autumn as a job of work rather than for show, and it is enjoyed as an occasion by all.

The reality of the steam engine's coming to agriculture was that the dawn to dusk agrarian society changed with the steam engine and the call of the whistle to mark shift changes – a horse got tired, the engine didn't. A horse needed feeding – in fact one needed three horses to cover the work of one; one to do the work, one to rest, and the other to be ill or incapacitated – so a steam engine became a desirable commodity. Many chroniclers of agricultural history dismiss steam power in agriculture as a heavy and expensive failure. The numbers of people employed in the census as 'agricultural machine proprietor/attendant' over the decades from the 1870s to 1940s would suggest otherwise, along with the production of many thousands of threshing machines and traction engines by English manufacturers, even when allowing for the massive export market, which would fill a separate book by itself.

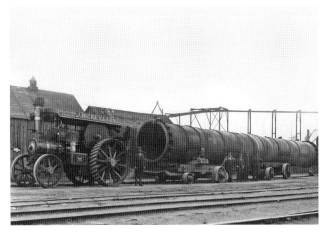

Another example of J. Hickey & Sons using *City of London*, moving a large pressure vessel. The length of the load requires two bogies to enable it to be manoeuvred through streets and roads to gain access to the delivery site. Fortunately the engine has survived in to preservation.

Working with steam was labour intensive. Although this is a 2016 recreation of steam sawing, with the team dressed as soldiers and prisoners of war, it gives a reasonable impression in the twenty-first century of what it must have been like.

Steam was very much part of the everyday scene – in this Bioscope (cinema) the engine – a Garrett 4CD tractor – is made a feature of at the front of the attraction. It's now part of the Hollycombe Collection in Hampshire where visitors can experience a steam fairground at first hand.

Burrell scenic showman's engine No.1 was owned by Pat Collins and was one of the last working steam engines on the fairground, lasting until the 1950s.

Steam continued commercially into the 1960s. Dredging silt to maintain open water at Sling Pool in the Clent Hills, Romsley, Worcestershire, was something that only steam could do for the National Trust on 23 June 1966. Operated by M. A. Brown, Tettenhall, Staffordshire, the two engines involved were Fowler K7 ploughing engines.

Fowler ploughing engines laid up at Bomford & Carr, Binton, 11 August 1968 – ironically the same day that the last steam-hauled train was operated on British Railways.

7

Saving Steam: The Preservation of Traction Engines

Keeping road steam vehicles for posterity has been around for many years. Perhaps the earliest example is that of the *Fardier à vapeur* of Nicolas Cugnot from 1771, mentioned in the first chapter, which by 1800 had been given a place in Paris' Musée des Arts et Métiers where it remains today. In the UK, William Murdoch's 1784 steam carriage model is the first British steam road vehicle in a museum – Birmingham's 'ThinkTank' – but for active live steam preservation, one has to move forward to the twentieth century.

Prior to the Second World War, we find a few privately owned engines in the ownership of the Honourable Peter Hoseason of Dowdeswell Court near Cheltenham. From 1937 to 1939 he acquired a number of old and interesting traction engines, but he was called up for war service in 1939 and all the engines bar one old Hornsby portable went for scrap. The portable became part of the Science Museum collection and is currently housed at Wroughton in Wiltshire. In 1937, what became the Road Locomotive Society was founded, but this as a learned society was more concerned with recording what it could about makes and makers before it was all too late – preservation in the active sense

Out to grass. Fowler compound traction engine 11708 at the premises of George Taylor, Redbourn, Herts, in May 1931. Taylor was a well-known dealer in engine; her fate was to be scrap as with so many engines that passed through his hands.

was yet to take off; even railway preservation, so often the big brother of the steam world, was mainly about recording, with only one locomotive privately saved in 1927 – *Gladstone* – and that was statically displayed at the then-York Railway Museum. Engines were cheap, and the concept of keeping an obsolete piece of machinery was not one that had universal appeal.

After the Second World War, more private owners began to rescue engines and look at steaming them for pleasure. The war had seen thousands of engines broken up for the war effort, but as pieces of machinery that were obsolete they could still be picked up for next to nothing. The late Ian Fraser of Arbroath bought a Marshall steam tractor in 1947, had it put back into steam, and used to go for Saturday morning jaunts around town with it until the sea coal he had acquired ran out, at which time the engine would be put to bed. He kept it at his home and, later on, it was to be the subject of a legal battle – 'The Arbroath Affair', which established the precedent for keeping a steam engine for pleasure on one's own property. The tractor later became part of the Leicestershire Museum collection where for a time it was in the care of the author, and it now can be seen in steam in the Midlands at various events.

Did you know?

In Kent in the 1940s and 1950s, Chris Lambert of Horsmonden had a collection of upwards of forty engines when the fashion was to get rid of them, and he held regular steam-ups of what he called his 'old gentlemen' in his yard. Enthusiasts from all across the country attended.

Preserved in Scotland by Ian Fraser in 1947, Marshall *Jingling Geordie* was on display at the now-closed Snibston Museum in July 2015. It has now been lent to a local steam enthusiast and is now back in steam.

Originally preserved by the Road Locomotive Society in 1951, Aveling traction engine 721 is now seen by thousands each year at the Science Museum, South Kensington, in London.

Saving steam engines in the immediate post-war years was very much the preserve of people working in isolation, and not many were aware of each other. The Road Locomotive Society did get involved in preservation in a limited way, acquiring an elderly Aveling & Porter traction engine and presenting it to the Science Museum in 1951, where it remains to this day, but that was all.

The Story of the National Traction Engine Trust – How It All Began
A national body looking to promote steam preservation was still far off when the now-famous Arthur Napper and his friend Miles Chetwynd-Stapleton bought engines for their pleasure in 1949; Arthur realising that one day none would be left if he hadn't preserved one. Berkshire thus became another place where individuals did something, but the stage was set for the next move. Arthur and Miles teased each other about their engines' ability and Miles set the challenge for a race in July 1950 for a firkin of ale to go to the winner. The rest is now history: Arthur's Marshall *Old Timer* beat Miles' Aveling *Ladygrove* in front of a group of locals – some twenty-five or so in number – at Appleford in Oxfordshire. There matters might have remained had Miles not asked for a rematch, by which time the local newspaper caught hold of the story. Thus, in August 1950, the Marshall beat the Aveling once more in front of some 2–300 people, one of whom was a reporter from the *Daily Mirror* and the story went national. This alerted others who had an interest in engines,

one of whom, 'Doc' Giles Romanes, was still involved until his death in 2016. He met Arthur and the pair had another race in 1951, by which time over a thousand people attended and the seeds of gatherings of steam engines were sown.

Did you know?

Doc Romanes, one of the pioneers of steam preservation, was a Harley Street eye surgeon in London, eminent in his field. His colleagues were so bemused by his steam engine hobby that they considered getting him medical help to overcome the interest! Mercifully, he was allowed to continue and even drove his engine over Tower Bridge on occasions.

The engine that started it all, Marshall 37690 *Old Timer* at the 1965 Appleford rally when still owned by Arthur Napper.

Appleford, 16 July 1967, saw this Wallis & Steevens agricultural engine No. 7683 carrying the name *Eileen the Erring*, when owned by Frank Upton. Earlier in preservation, the engine had been owned by Giles Romanes who gave it the name after a brush with the law. The plate on the side of the boiler shows it saw service for the Hampshire War Agricultural Committee on threshing duties during the Second World War.

This 7 N.H.P. Wallis & Steevens Expansion agricultural engine of 1916 is taking on water at the Banbury Steam Engine Fair held at Bloxham Fields near Banbury on 28 June 1969 when owned by E. G. Evans of Bicester, Oxon.

Going back a little, in 1893 a professional organisation to protect the rights of steam road users was formed, which became the National Traction Engine and Tractor Association Incorporated. This fought the corner of traction engine users across the country who faced all manner of issues from smoke emissions to taxation and speeding, of all matters. This encompassed threshing machine users and steam cultivation associations ultimately, but by the 1950s was an institution in the same decline as the engines and users it sought to assist. Very few were using engines commercially at this date, and legal harassment of those that did was much less than it had been when the Association was set up.

In 1952, the then-Secretary of the Association, Frank Stephens, heard of the happenings at Appleford, and went to see Arthur Napper. Maybe he was hoping for a boost to the Association, but he assisted Arthur in organising a gathering of engines on 8 June that year. Still branded as a race, five engines competed and four were displayed, but after that year no more races were held due to concern about ageing flywheels bursting under the strain of race conditions. Future years saw demonstrations of engine driving skill, and much longer events rather than flat-out five-minute matters, and the concept of the traction engine rally as we know it was born.

Stephens and his Association continued to support the scene throughout 1953 and 1954, but they were still a professional body with salaried staff such as Stephens himself. The men preserving the engines as a hobby felt that an organisation that reflected the voluntary nature of the movement was needed and, thus, in May 1954, seven people gathered at the home of

Like attracts like, and enthusiasts gathered in fields and yards across the country to enjoy their engines. This is Eric Middleton's yard at Hartlebury on 6 April 1969.

Alastair Dacre Lacy and formed the National Traction Engine Club, whose 60th anniversary was celebrated in 2014. It was agreed to publish a magazine, with the Appleford gathering being the main club event. By then, the appeal of engines was spreading across the country, and local rallies such as the one at Pickering in North Yorkshire began to be established, as did local clubs.

The National Traction Engine Club began to be concerned with working with a modern preservation movement, and became involved with safety, legal, and insurance issues relating to road steam vehicles, as well as publicity and raising the profile of the steam engine. Yet in its infancy, it came very close to folding completely. We are used to the problems of running steam rallies and outdoor events in the rain these days, but the other costs of running a national club were new to the team running the organisation and, of course, no-one had done it before to give them any clue as to what to expect. The receipts from the rallies were often shared with charitable causes and, whilst laudable, this and the cost of producing a quality magazine meant that by 1957 the club's finances were in a parlous state. Nearing bankruptcy, the committee had a meeting on 21 August that year to consider options, one of which was to wind the club up, as it was £88 in the red – a large amount in those days.

During the meeting, the atmosphere changed from despair to optimism as the idea of holding a raffle for funds was mooted. Then the prize was discussed, and the Treasurer, Walter Edney, offered to present a Wallis & Steevens traction engine of his as first prize. He personally took out an overdraft of £100 to tide the club over and then paid expenses to all engine owners who had been at the 1957 event. The gamble paid off, and the club went thereafter from strength to strength. With the growth of rallies across the country, the last Appleford National Rally was held in 1971, but a 21st anniversary road run was started from Appleford in 1975; ensuring the place had made its mark in history due to the efforts of Arthur Napper and the NTEC. In 2004, the village sign for Appleford had a traction engine image placed on it to commemorate five decades since that first wager for ale.

Events and the world change and the club moved on. It acquired charitable status and, reflecting that, changed its name to the National Traction Engine Trust in the 1980s, which it now operates under. This gives a certain degree of gravitas after six decades – amusing when

Some rallies were in an urban setting. McLaren No. 127 was a regular attender at the Newhall Street Rallies, organised by the Science Museum in Birmingham, on this occasion 18 May 1969. At this time, the 1882 engine was owned by John Mayes of Eccleshall, Staffordshire.

Early in the 1960s there grew a desire to show engines and equipment doing the jobs they were built for. An event that grew out of this was the Stratford on Avon Edwardian fair, this being the 1969 one. *The Ballie* – a Burrell showman's road locomotive built in 1911 – is providing power for a 98-key Marenghi fairground organ just to the right. The organ was once owned by Pat Collins of Walsall.

The Town & Country Festival was for many years an annual event that included a rally at the National Agricultural Centre at Stoneleigh in Warwickshire. This 1983 picture was taken from the commentary box and shows a typical selection of engines in the arena during the grand parade.

The Brading Experience engine collection has now been closed and sold, but there are a number of museums and attractions around the country where engines can be seen at close quarters without fear of getting dirty.

Engines have been film stars, perhaps the best known being Fowler showman's engine *The Iron Maiden*, which is seen all across the country, here in 2007 at Masham. The engine has travelled extensively across the UK and Europe – such is its fame.

one considers that those activities of the early days were looked at askance by such groups as the Institute of Mechanical Engineers.

From the humble beginnings in Appleford, the steam rally or vintage gathering has become a regular fixture across the country on weekends throughout the spring, summer and autumn. Gatherings of engines began to include other exhibits, such as fairground rides, miniature engines and model displays along with a supporting cast of cars, tractors and such like. Some of the rallies have been carrying on for over six decades now, such as the Bedford club show and the West of England Steam Engine Society event. Others have come and gone, such as the Tom Rolt Vintage Rally, which was run by the author and friends for a number of years in support of the Talyllyn Railway in Mid Wales.

Rallies vary in size and theme. In the early 1960s, the White Waltham steam fair showed how engines could still drive fairgrounds and demonstrated what they were used for. Not long afterwards, in 1969, a 'Great Working of Steam Engines' was organised at Stourpaine Bushes in Dorset, where engines were showcased driving threshing machines, sawing timber, hauling loads, and generally doing the jobs they were built for. So successful was this event that it grew into the 'Great Dorset Steam Fair', which still runs to this day – now based at Tarrant Hinton near Blandford Forum, where it has become known as the National Heritage Show. Every year nearly 300 engines attend, and the showman's engine line-up at night is a spectacle to behold. The emphasis is on action, where ploughing takes place across several acres and an area known as the 'Play Pen' is set aside for steam haulage demonstrations up and downhill, which is perhaps the greatest show of steam power in the UK, whether road or rail based! For a week, the show site becomes the third-largest settlement in Dorset, and thousands from across the world make the annual trip.

Of course, there are rallies all across the country, not just Dorset, and they range from small country shows where one or two engines may be present, to established events such as the County of Salop Steam Engine Society show where over eighty engines will be present – both on static display and at work. Informal steam parties, road runs and gatherings are less formal but no less fun for many, and provide the opportunity to share engines with family and friends, and sometimes new audiences – especially if a pub is involved. Whilst drink-driving laws still apply and enginemen comply with that, the convivial atmosphere of a village hostelry and three or four engines is hard to beat.

It can thus be seen that the preservation of traction engines has a long and illustrious history, and shows every sign of continuing. The world has changed around us a lot over the last sixty years since steam engines ceased to be a common sight on the farms and roads of the UK, but the appeal of the traction engine in all its facets endures. There are some 3,000 or more engines in preservation in the UK now, listed in the regularly updated 'Traction Engine

Perhaps the greatest spectacle of steam power in the UK – heavy haulage at the Great Dorset Steam Fair where engines and loads are pitted against a gradient in an area known as the Playpen and, yes, the ground does shake!

Register'; a number of these are steam rollers and steam wagons, but the figures tell their own story. Even in 2017, engines are being imported from other parts of the world and it is thought that there may still be more engines in the UK that have yet to be found and enter preservation than is generally known. Remains have been found in streams, in coal mines, on top of Welsh mountains, and even two engines were recovered from the shores of Loch Ness! The enthusiasm for recovering and restoring steam knows no bounds!

8
What Now?

Why Preserve a Traction Engine?

The steam engine is one of the few inventions where it has been created purely for good, not to drop bombs on people or blow them up – so said the late Revd Teddy Boston, himself the saviour of a Foster traction engine, *Fiery Elias*, which became a coal-fired pulpit on occasion at rallies. Others have said that it is the nearest thing that man has made to a living creature – feed it and it becomes alive, warm and breathes. It has an appeal quite unlike anything else; it smells, it tastes, and it responds to human touch. It's elemental and takes time to come to life; it cannot just be turned on or off. A steam engine has history, craftsmanship, aesthetic appeal – it excites the young and inspires wistful nostalgia in the old, though those who can remember it working for a living are now few and far between. Standing next to a showman's engine working hard on a fairground at night with 300 amps showing on the ammeter as the engine drives a ride is something that touches all the senses except taste in a way that words cannot describe adequately – it has to be experienced!

The preservation of steam engines now goes back over seventy years and some engines have been with their heritage owners far longer than they were in their commercial existence. Some owners enjoy an engine for a time, then sell it and buy another. Others get involved, buy an engine, and keep it for many years. As the interest has grown, enthusiasts began to build model and miniature engines; beginning to recreate machines that no longer exist in many cases. This has recently developed into full-size new builds of engine designs and the re-appearance of famous names that were once thought long lost.

FE 9179

One of the characters in the traction engine world was the Revd Teddy Boston of Market Bosworth, Leicestershire. His engine was a Foster agricultural engine of 1927 carrying the name *Fiery Elias* – a biblical link to the Old Testament. It spent most of its working life in Lincolnshire, before preservation.

Marshall traction engine *Peggie* after recovery by the Scourfield family from dereliction in Pembrokeshire, Dorset, September 2015. A long task of restoration lies ahead, but the end result will be worth it.

Atmosphere! A Burrell showman's engine is seen generating and providing light after dark at the 2015 Great Dorset Steam Fair.

2016 saw significant progress on Fowler road locomotive *Talisman*, undergoing reconstruction at Bouth in Cumbria. This engine had vanished into obscurity for decades and was acquired as little more than a pile of pieces and a boiler.

Models and Miniatures

If the lure of live steam beckons, but you don't have the time or skill to build an engine from scratch, then kits of castings and parts are available, or even fully machined kits where all that is needed are simple hand tools and enthusiasm. A steam fix is even possible within the comfort of one's own home through the small models and toys that can be bought complete, like the famous Mamod and Wilesco models. One of the latter was your author's introduction to live steam, running around his parents' kitchen floor. Over thirty years later, although I now have access to full size historic engines, my daughters and I still enjoy the thrill of steaming up one of these little engines and playing with it in the back yard of our house. Steam is truly accessible to all now; there are even gatherings and rallies held for toy steam engines if that be your passion. If you still don't fancy live steam, some really good static models can be bought to display around the home, made by Corgi, Oxford Die-Cast, and Midsummer Models.

Some engine aficionados build up collections of traction engines, equipment and ephemera. Other enthusiasts cannot afford to have an engine, so lend a hand with restoration and running of an engine. Many enjoy photography, history or visiting rallies, and the interest covers all walks of life. Engineers rub shoulders with surgeons, for the second member of the National Traction Engine Trust, the aforementioned Giles Romanes, was an eminent Harley Street eye specialist.

The future of steam is in their hands – steam apprentices giving a lesson to the President of the National Traction Engine Trust, Andrew Semple, in September 2014 at the Trust's 60th anniversary event.

Records and Research

Records and historic images can be found in many County Record Offices, and the Museum of English Rural Life in Reading is a Mecca for those wanting to undertake serious research into engines, their uses and past. (https://www.reading.ac.uk/TheMERL)

The business archives of a number of engineering firms are there, and a number are also at the Lincolnshire Record Office, due to the great concentration of firms in that county (https://www.lincolnshire.gov.uk/libraries-and-archives/lincolnshire-archives/).

You may also wish to seek out the sites of where engines worked or were built for a real challenge. Fowlers' vast site is now a supermarket car park, whilst others are marked with blue plaques or, sadly, not at all.

Most Record Offices now have digitised images available on line and sites such as 'Windows on Warwickshire' will repay a quick search on the term 'traction engine' with hundreds of fascinating pictures.

From one business it is possible to buy prints of traction engines made from the original printing blocks used in maker's catalogues from over a century ago in a real link with the past. (http://www.gonetopress.com/index.htm)

Steam at home; the Gone To Press framed print of a McLaren compound traction engine – just the picture to go on your wall!

The National Traction Engine Trust

The Trust exists for all who have an interest in traction engines, but its mission statement is 'Preserving our Heritage with Steam on the Road'. Rallies are important, but many still derive enjoyment from driving their engines upon the Queen's highway. Thus the Trust keeps an eye on legislation that may affect the engine owner and driver, from the use of fire hydrants to the correct driving licence to operate a road roller. It has members looking after technical developments, insurance issues – running a very successful insurance disc scheme for many years now – and a Rally Authorisation Unit. The latter offers guidance notes for the operation of safe and legal rallies. The Rally Organisers and Engine Owners' sections also hold annual conferences to discuss current matters and good practice, often asking external speakers to come and talk about related issues, such as the legality of towing trailers.

An Engine Owner's Code of Practice helps novices and old hands alike, and with the novices in mind, the Trust runs an Annual Training Weekend and Driving Course, which initially gave hands on experience and now leads to a three-year syllabus should students wish to follow that. Recognising that financially not all can afford to attend, it now also offers bursaries to allow members of lesser means to take part – a laudable part of the enterprise. Moving on from that, the Trust also offers a voluntary Certificate of Competency scheme, whereby engine crew can be assessed on their abilities and coached on improving their engine handling skills – a very valuable aspect, as those who worked commercially with engines are getting fewer and fewer, and skills retention is a very important part of preserving the heritage. (https://www.ntet.co.uk)

Above: A driver training course from the National Traction Engine Trust allows students to work their way up to taking an engine out on the road for a run, such as with Foster *Sprig* here, near Astwood Bank, on the 2015 course.

Below: Steam on the Road is celebrated by the National Traction Engine Trust on 'Steam it Sunday'; an annual event on the first Sunday of October. Fowler road loco *Providence* is seen in 2016 making its way to the first of these events, which encourage people to enjoy steam engines in action from models up to full size.

Hydrant training! An activity of the National Traction Engine Trust is to encourage best practice and responsible use of the road – this includes taking on water when out and about.

A Steam Club Near You?

Across the country, there are many local and regional steam societies and clubs, from the Bon Accord Steam Society in Aberdeen and surrounding areas, to the West of England Steam Engine Society in Devon & Cornwall. Other interest societies exist on a national basis, such as the Road Locomotive Society and the Steam Plough Club – both long-established in their own right. Road runs are regular parts of the steam season – both organised ones by clubs and more ad hoc ones with groups of friends. The steam hobby is a broad church united by the word 'fun'.

Steam on Show

Since the 1960s, a number of steam museums and collections have been established. Some still exist, others have closed or been dispersed. Perhaps the best known are Strumpshaw (http://www.strumpshawsteammuseum.co.uk/) and Bressingham in Norfolk (http://www.bressingham.co.uk/home.aspx), though a pleasing feature of the last thirty years has been the rise of museums based on the products of specific manufacturers, such as the Charles Burrell Museum in Thetford (http://www.thecharlesburrellmuseum.com/), and the Garrett Museum in Leiston (http://www.longshopmuseum.co.uk/).

Lincolnshire celebrates its past with the Museum of Lincolnshire Life covering all the major firms (https://www.lincolnshire.gov.uk/heritage-and-tourism/museum-of-lincolnshire-life/), whilst in the South there is a centre in Tavistock based on Robey products (http://www.therobeytrust.co.uk/) and, in Basingstoke, the Milestones Museum devotes large parts to the companies of Tasker and Wallis & Steevens (https://hampshireculturaltrust.org.uk/milestones-museum).

Live steam working in both agricultural and fairground settings is to be found at the Hollycombe Working Steam Museum in Hampshire, and a full steaming day is to be recommended. (http://www.hollycombe.co.uk)

A number of other museums and collections show engines or a single engine, and these locations can be found in Barrie C. Woods' *Traction Engine Museum Guide.* (http://www.stpublications.co.uk/showbook.php?bookid=153)

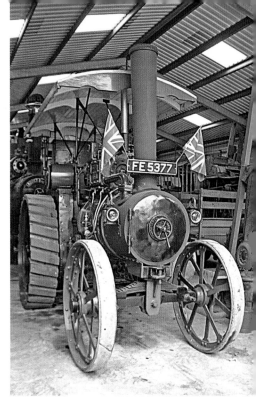

Right: The Robey Trust based in Tavistock, Devon, have gathered a collection of Robey products; this is an example of an engine reconstructed from a 1923 roller seen at their premises, which are open to visit on selected days (although not an established museum as-such).

Below: This 1905 Burrell road locomotive carrying the name *The President* is seen at Bressingham Gardens, Diss, Norfolk, when it was part of a collection of some fourteen engines amassed by the late Alan Bloom. The engine has since moved on to another collection north of the border but Bressingham remains an active and popular steam centre.

Read All About It

Traction engines figure more recently in children's stories, such as Trevor the Traction Engine in the Revd Wilbert Awdry's Railway Series – more often known as the Thomas the Tank Engine books. A number of owners have presented their preserved engines as 'Trevor' at events where Thomas and friends are present, and for several years many children's first experience of an engine has been at such an event. Val Biro who created the 'Gumdrop' vintage car series of stories also incorporated a Fowler traction engine, *The Farmer's Friend*, into the tales and it was that which I recall in my formative years – another publication worth seeking out, for it is very enjoyable yet completely authentic in all details of the story and the vehicles contained therein!

In adult literature, Fred Archer, a farmer from the Vale of Evesham, chronicled country life in the twentieth century as he knew it; writing at least one book of recollections a year. Most of these contained at least one or two memories and stories of steam working on the land, from being shown for sale at agricultural shows, to the spectacle of commercial steam ploughing hard into the autumn to make sure that the land was ready. Even the title of one of his books – *Golden Sheaves, Black Horses* – refers to steam engines working at threshing time. The traction engine is embedded in popular culture throughout the decades it was in use and beyond to the present day. Slightly differently, the alternative history novel *Pavane* by Keith Roberts describes in one of its sections a vivid account of working a Burrell road haulage locomotive across Dorset – in 1968! Seek it out if that sparks the imagination.

Away from fiction, there are dozens of more in-depth books on traction engines if this slim volume has sparked your interest. There are albums of historic photographs, selections of recent colour images, reminiscences of working with engines, and detailed histories of manufacturers and operators. One can buy a book with guidelines on how to look-after and drive a traction engine and also others where one can learn the intricacies of the single crank compounding system of a Burrell engine; such is the breadth of literature available. A very comprehensive list of all engines in the country has been published every four years or so since the late 1960s as the *Traction Engine Register* (http://thetractionengineregister.webs.com/). Many traction engine books are available second-hand, whilst most titles currently in print can be bought from the sales officer of the National Traction Engine Trust (http://www.ntet.co.uk/shop).

On the high street, two glossy magazines are available – *Old Glory* (http://www.oldglory. co.uk/) & *Vintage Spirit* (https://www.vintagespirit.co.uk/).

Both are published monthly and celebrate vintage preservation and cover historic features too, but concentrate particularly on the traction engine and the people involved in rallies and preservation. One could do worse than pick up one of these for a good browse.

In the virtual world, the Traction-Talk website is the premier UK internet forum for the traction engine enthusiast, where owners, engineers, photographers, historians and others meet to ask questions, discuss, and show off their pride-and-joy online and across the world (http://www.tractiontalkforum.com/index.php). Traction-Talk's creator also runs the comprehensive Steam Scenes website, where he has set himself the challenge of photographing and digitising images of every surviving steam traction engine in the country and covers a national range of steam events (http:steamscenes.org.uk).

In the world of social media, the National Traction Engine Trust (https://www.ntet.co.uk) has an active Facebook and Twitter presence and the number of steam enthusiasts who share information and pictures in the virtual world is massive and international. That said, traction engines have a peculiarly English appeal and, whilst steam preservation is a big thing in America and parts of Europe, no-one is quite as passionate about steam engines as we are!

Above: August 2016 and Alan Sparkes' Fowler ploughing engine *Rusty* is seen at the Great Dorset Steam Fair with ploughing tackle in tow. Sun, steam and crowds – it doesn't get much better than this!
Below: Informal local gatherings sometimes bring out engines that don't often go to rallies – here a Ransomes and Fowler are seen in a pub car park at Tickhill in South Yorkshire, September 2008.

Fun and friendship in the world of steam; a September 2015 road run pauses at Swainby in North Yorkshire for lunch. All are welcome and the spectacle of engines on the road in the twenty-first century continues.